THE
UNITED STATES

SALLY GARRINGTON

Facts On File, Inc.

Facts On File, Inc.
132 West 31st Street
New York NY 10001

Library of Congress Cataloging-in-Publication-Data is on file with the publisher.

Facts On File books are available at special discounts when purchased in bulk quantities for businesses, associations, institutions, or sales promotions. Please call our Special Sales Department in New York at (212) 967-8800 or (800) 322-8755.

You can find Facts On File on the World Wide Web at http://www.factsonfile.com

Printed in China by Imago

10 9 8 7 6 5 4 3 2 1

Editor:	Polly Goodman
Designer:	Jane Hawkins
Picture research:	Lynda Lines
Map artwork:	Peter Bull
Charts and graphs:	Alex Pang

Endpapers (front):	Rock formations in Monument Valley, on the Arizona/Utah border.
Title page:	High-rise hotels on Miami Beach, Florida.
Imprint and Contents page:	Mountains, lakes and forests in the Grand Teton National Park, Wyoming.
Endpapers (back):	A marina in Honolulu, the capital city and main port of Hawaii.

First published by Evans Brothers Limited, 2A Portman Mansions, Chiltern Street, London W1U 6NR, United Kingdom

This edition published under license from Evans Brothers Limited. All rights reserved.

CONTENTS

The US flag.

INTRODUCING THE UNITED STATES

A view over the Grand Canyon National Park, in Arizona.

The United States is the wealthiest and most powerful country in the world. Much of its wealth is due to its size, and the diversity of its landscapes and people. Although only independent since 1776, it has become the most influential country in the world. People from many lands have migrated to the United States to begin a new life, joining the Native Americans who have lived on the American continent for thousands of years.

The United States consists of 50 states, 48 of which adjoin each other. Two states are separate from the rest. Alaska lies to the west of Canada and is the largest of the states. Hawaii is a group of volcanic islands in the Pacific Ocean.

A COUNTRY OF CONTRASTS

The United States is so big that there is a variety of climates, from the subtropical regions of Florida to the cooler, northern climates around New England. Its size also has an effect on local time. Across the 48 states there are four time zones, which means that when it is midnight in California, it is already

KEY DATA

Area:	9,629,091km²
Highest Point:	Mt McKinley, Alaska (6,194m)
Lowest Point:	Death Valley, California (–86m)
Population:	280.6 million (2000)
Birth rate per 1,000:	14.5 (2000)
Death rate per 1,000:	8.8 (2000)
GDP per Capita:	$35,510*
Currency:	USDollar($)
Capital City:	Washington, District of Columbia
Major Cities:	New York (pop. 7.3 million)
	Los Angeles (pop. 3.6 million)
	Chicago (pop. 2.8 million)
Number of States:	50

* Calculated on Purchasing Power Parity basis
Source: *US Census and American Factfinder*

3 a.m. in New York. In Alaska, which is in a time zone behind California, it would be 11p.m. the previous evening.

Most Americans live in urban areas, but huge open landscapes are used for recreation, and to escape the pressures of urban living. Some of these landscapes, such as the Grand Canyon, are among the most spectacular in the world.

Americans have the highest standard of living in the world. As a nation, Americans consume 25 percent of the world's energy, yet the country only has about 5 percent of the world's population.

American influence has spread to most parts of the world, often through successful films and television shows. The nation's restaurant chains can now be found in towns and cities in all corners of the globe.

Right: Football is an exciting team sport, played mainly in the United States and Canada.

LANDSCAPE AND CLIMATE

The rocky cliffs of Big Sur, California, on the west coast of the United States.

The country's mainland (not including Alaska) can be divided into three major regions: a mountainous area in the west, highlands in the east and plains in the middle. In the west, the Rocky Mountains include several peaks over 4,270m high. The Great Plains of the interior are mostly below 400m. In the east are the Appalachian Mountains, which include the Blue Ridge Mountains. A coastal plain runs down the east of the country and around the Gulf of Mexico, including the delta of the Mississippi River. The mostly low-lying eastern and southern coastline includes many barrier islands and spits.

CASE STUDY
MOUNT ST HELENS ERUPTION

A cloud of ash rises from the top of Mount St Helens on 18 May, 1980.

Mount St Helens is a volcano in the Cascade Mountains. Here, the Juan de Fuca Plate is drawn beneath the North American Plate. In April 1980, a bulge appeared on the northern side of the volcano. On 18 May, an earthquake measuring 5.0 on the Richter scale caused a landslide. A massive explosion of gas and steam was followed by a towering ash cloud a few seconds later. An area of more than 500km^2 was devastated, with forests flattened by the blast and areas covered in a thick layer of ash. Although a devastating blow to the immediate plant and animal life, the volcano's eruption has brought new sources of nutrients to the surface, which, over time, will benefit the soils of the region.

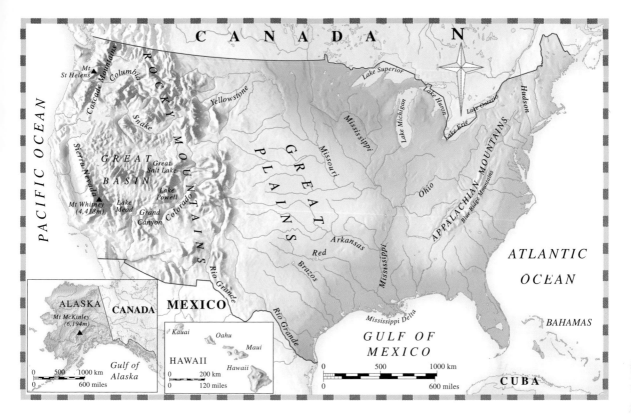

Rocky shores lie along the west coast and the coast of Alaska. The resistant rocks form features such as headlands, arches and stacks. The land is constantly being changed by the forces of wind and water. Below the earth's surface there are other forces at work. Along the western side of the United States, there are several plate boundaries. These mark the edges of the large plates that make up the earth's surface. Extreme heat within the earth sets up huge convection currents, which move the plates toward, away and past each other depending on the direction of flow.

CASE STUDY
THE NORTHRIDGE EARTHQUAKE

In California, the North American Plate and the Pacific Plate move next to each other within the San Andreas Fault System. Along certain sections, these plates lock together due to friction. Pressure builds up until one plate suddenly moves forward, causing an earthquake.

On 17 January 1994, an earthquake measuring 6.7 on the Richter scale occurred under the heavily populated suburb of Northridge, in Los Angeles. Even though California has invested heavily in earthquake-resistant buildings, there was a great deal of damage and 57 deaths. The damage was greater than expected because the epicenter of the earthquake was directly beneath the suburb. Many of the buildings damaged were older structures, built without earthquake-resistant designs. A stretch of elevated highway collapsed when the reinforced concrete gave way. It was here that most of the deaths occurred. Authorities are currently trying to ensure that older buildings are upgraded with earthquake-resistant materials, and imposing stricter regulations on highway construction in order to be better prepared for the next movement of the earth.

AMERICAN RIVERS AND THEIR LANDFORMS

The United States has several large river systems, including the Mississippi in the east, the Columbia in the northwest and the Colorado in the southwest. The sources of the rivers are usually in upland areas. The source of the Columbia River is in the ice fields of the Canadian Rockies, whereas the Arkansas River, a tributary of the Mississippi, begins near Leadville, Colorado, in the US Rocky Mountains.

Each river drains an area known as its drainage basin. The Mississippi's drainage basin covers 41 percent of the nation's total land area. In some parts of the country, rivers do not flow all year round. Rivers such as the San Gabriel in California are reduced to a trickle or nothing at all for part of the year.

Rivers alter the landscape in two ways: by erosion and by deposition.

EROSION

Erosion is more important in the upper sections of a river. Here, vertical erosion cuts down into the river bed, forming a V-shaped valley with steep sides. During heavy rainfall, material is washed down from the valley sides and adds to the river's load. The rock-covered river bed makes the flow uneven or turbulent. The river winds its way around areas of highland, which form interlocking spurs.

Many of these landscapes can be seen in the Rocky Mountains. In the upper section of the Arkansas River, in Colorado, the river drops 3,000m in just 200km. Here there are waterfalls and rapids that are also typical of the upper reaches of a river.

Gorges can be formed when there is a change in sea or land level. The Grand Canyon was formed many millions of years ago, when movements lifted the Colorado Plateau. As the plateau rose, the Colorado River cut down through it, carving out the deep gorge of the Grand Canyon.

TRANSPORTATION

Rivers carry material in different ways. Larger material is dragged along the river bed while finer material is carried in the water. The Colorado's name means 'red-colored' because it has been so colored by the sediment in the water. Rivers erode their banks and beds with the material they carry; the faster a river flows, the more material it carries and the quicker it erodes.

DEPOSITION

In the lower sections of a river, deposition is the main process. The slope is gentler and rivers tend to move across their flood plains in a series of bends, called meanders. Within the

Riding the rapids over Hosum Falls on the White Salmon River, in Washington state.

meanders, erosion takes place at the outer edges and the river widens by lateral (sideways) erosion. Deposition occurs on the inside of a bend where the flow of water is slower. The neck of a meander can sometimes become so narrow that eventually the river cuts across the neck instead of flowing around the meander. The meander is then abandoned and forms an oxbow lake. There are many oxbow lakes on the Mississippi flood plain in Louisiana. Eagle Lake, on the Louisiana-Missouri border, was known as Eagle Bend until the river took a short cut across the neck of the meander and created a lake.

Sometimes rivers overflow their banks and deposit material on the flood plain. The coarsest material is dropped first and forms a natural embankment, called a levee.

Estuaries, such as the Roanoke River estuary in North Carolina, form where a river meets the sea. As the speed of the river slows down, it drops some of the material it is carrying. If this material blocks the main channel, the river is forced to flow around it in a number of small distributaries. If the ocean currents are not strong enough to remove material faster than it is being deposited, a delta is formed. The Mississippi Delta, in Louisiana, forms where the Mississippi meets the Gulf of Mexico.

The Mississippi, the country's longest river, meanders across its flood plain.

THE MISSISSIPPI COMPARED

River:	Mississippi	Nile	Amazon	Yangtze	Ganges
Continent:	North America	Africa	South America	Asia	Asia
Length, including tributaries (km):	6,019	6,484	6,516	5,800	2,700
Drainage area (km^2):	4,160	2,881	7,180	1,970	1,073
Source:	NW Minnesota	Lake Tana	Andes	Tibetan Plateau	Himalayas

Source: *River Systems of the World* (www.rev.net)

MANAGEMENT OF THE MISSISSIPPI

The Mississippi Delta is steadily becoming more salty. This affects the region's farmlands.

The Mississippi is the largest river system in the United States, with 250 tributaries including the great Missouri River. It drains 31 states and carries 400 million tonnes of sediment down to the Gulf of Mexico each year. The river provides water for drinking and irrigation to towns along its banks and is the most important transport waterway in the nation.

The Mississippi's wide flood plain has been developed for agriculture and settlement. The river has been managed to improve flood control, water storage and navigation.

The Mississippi Delta is one of the largest in the world, but it is shrinking. Now that river management methods (see below) have partially controlled the flooding, less sediment

METHODS OF RIVER MANAGEMENT

Method	Action
Dams	Contain surplus flow to control flooding. Store water for irrigation and domestic use.
Concrete levees	Protect vulnerable towns from flooding. These replace earth levees.
Removal of bankside vegetation	Makes water flow faster so the river is less likely to flood.
Control of dikes	Channels fastest flow into the center of the river, decreasing the chance of flooding.
Removal of meanders	Reduces river's length and straightens channel so it is less likely to flood. Helps navigation.
Spillways	Divert excess water away from major cities to a lake.

Source: US Corps of Engineers; American Rivers (www.americanrivers.org)

is being added to its flood plain and delta. At its mouth, waves in the Gulf of Mexico remove material from the delta, and salt water is now moving in, destroying farmland.

Development along the river has caused several problems. Urban areas use the river to dispose of their domestic and industrial wastes yet need the river as a water supply. Some stretches of the Mississippi are heavily polluted. Oil and gas extraction in the delta has also caused pollution. This has damaged some of the plants and animals that live there.

Farmers along the river have had to use chemical fertilizers to enrich their soils, because their land no longer receives sediment from the river floods. Excess nitrates from these fertilizers are washed into the river, causing algae and other plants to grow. The plants use up oxygen in the water, so there is not enough for animal life in the river. Farmers have also drained wetlands next to the river to increase their area of production. This means that when the river does flood, there is no natural use land to absorb the excess water.

CASE STUDY
THE MISSISSIPPI FLOODS OF 1993

In 1993, heavy rains fell in intense thunderstorms in the Midwest. An area the size of England was flooded at the point where the Ohio River meets the Mississippi, and more than 1,000 levees collapsed. Most of the government-built, concrete levees that protected the larger towns held firm, but 80 percent of the earth levees failed. In total there were 50 deaths, and 75,000 people had to be evacuated from their homes. Huge areas of crops were destroyed. The floods caught people by surprise. The construction of the levees and other flood-control measures had made people feel safe, so large amounts of new housing and industry had been built on the flood plain. People felt so secure that many did not own household insurance, and were thus left with nothing when their homes were destroyed in the floods.

In April 2001 another flood hit the Mississippi basin, the fourth serious flood since the disaster of 1993, making it clear that engineering methods alone cannot

This road, in the state of Iowa, was closed by serious floods in 1993.

prevent floods, and that flood-control methods need to work with the river processes, not against them. Recently there have been moves toward restoring some of the river's meanders to slow its flow. In some areas, plans are in place to prevent further development on the flood plain. Farmers are being paid to allow some of their land to serve as wetlands, so that if the river overflows again, the wetland areas will act like sponges and absorb some of the excess water.

CLIMATES OF THE USA

The United States is so large that it has a wide range of climates, from subtropical in the southeast, to Arctic tundra in the north.

COASTAL CLIMATES

Climates near the coasts are the least extreme because they are influenced by the oceans. In the southeast, around Florida, the climate is subtropical, with warm temperatures all year round and minimum monthly rainfalls of over 50mm. Vegetation is lush, with palm trees thriving. High humidity can make daily life uncomfortable, and there is a risk of hurricanes in the autumn, which often come ashore in this area.

In other warm southern and eastern coasts, the heat causes the buildup of cumulonimbus storm clouds, forming thunderstorms with heavy rain. All along the eastern coasts there is deciduous and coniferous woodland, depending on the soil type.

The west coast is drier in the south, with a more Mediterranean climate. California's warm, dry summers attract many residents. The natural vegetation has adapted to the summer drought and is a mix of scrub oak and drought-resistant shrubs.

Farther north on the west coast is the wettest region in the country. Wet, westerly winds from the Pacific Ocean are forced to rise over the mountains, droping their moisture as rain on the western slopes. Here the area is heavily forested with conifers.

INTERIOR CONTINENTAL CLIMATE

The interior of the United States has a large temperature range because the land heats and cools more rapidly farther away from the oceans. There is little rainfall because the area is in the rain shadow of the Rocky Mountains. Prairie grasses that can cope with the cold winters and lack of rainfall make up the natural vegetation. Tornadoes form over parts of this region because of the intense heat of the land.

DESERT CLIMATES

Desert climates are found in the southwest, in the rain shadow of the Rocky Mountains. Vegetation in this region has adapted to the climate. Cacti store water in their fleshy leaves, and other plants, such as blackbrush, have very small leaves to reduce water loss. Until very recently, these areas had low populations, but now cities such as Palm Springs and Las Vegas are attracting large numbers of people who enjoy the hot climate. Air conditioning and the availability of water make a high standard of living possible.

MOUNTAIN CLIMATES

In the western mountains the climate changes with the altitude. Deciduous woodland grows lower down, with tundra and snowcaps in the peaks. Small populations have long made a living from the timber industry, but tourism is becoming increasingly important to these mountain areas. Many towns serve as ski resorts in the winter and popular touring centers in the summer.

Waterfront houses in subtropical Miami.

CLIMATE ZONES

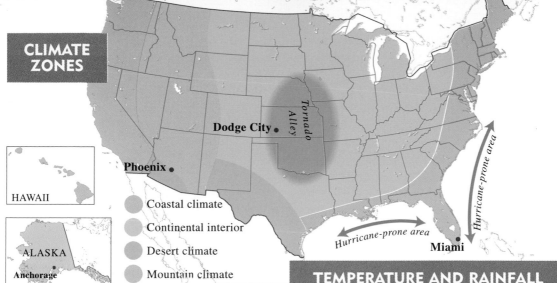

Dodge City

Tornado Alley

Phoenix

HAWAII

ALASKA

Anchorage

Miami

Hurricane-prone area

Hurricane-prone area

- Coastal climate
- Continental interior
- Desert climate
- Mountain climate
- Tundra

ARCTIC TUNDRA

Alaska has a tundra climate. The winters are very cold, but the southern coastal region can experience mild summers because a warm current flows past the area. The southern region has dense conifer forests, although the growing season lasts only five months. The north is too cold for trees to grow and the vegetation consists of mostly lichens and mosses. The ground never thaws out completely, which results in a permafrost layer. The larger centers of population in Alaska are in the warmer south.

The Grand Teton National Park, in north-west Wyoming, contains over 20 mountain peaks, each rising higher than 3,000m.

TEMPERATURE AND RAINFALL

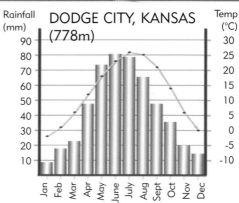

Rainfall (mm) — DODGE CITY, KANSAS (778m) — Temp (°C)

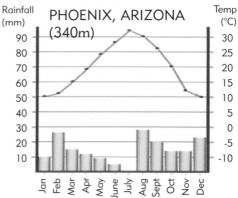

Rainfall (mm) — PHOENIX, ARIZONA (340m) — Temp (°C)

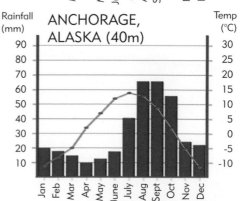

Rainfall (mm) — ANCHORAGE, ALASKA (40m) — Temp (°C)

KEY: Rainfall — Temperature

CLIMATIC HAZARDS

A climatic hazard is an extreme weather event that can threaten lives and property. The United States experiences a wide range of climatic hazards, including hurricanes, tornadoes, floods, droughts, blizzards and ice storms that kill a number of people each year. The US government spends a great deal of money researching these hazards in order to prevent future damage.

HURRICANES

Hurricanes are violent storms formed over warm oceans, around an area of very low pressure. As well as strong winds, they bring heavy rain, lightning and storm waves. The National Hurricane Center in Miami keeps a close watch on any tropical storms developing over the oceans, which might turn into hurricanes and move across the mainland. The Hurricane Center's predictions have become more accurate about the paths the hurricanes will take. Important information about weather systems is constantly being sent to the center from weather satellites orbiting the earth.

NUMBER OF DEATHS BY HAZARD IN THE UNITED STATES, 1994–98

Source: Federal Emergency Management Agency (FEMA); US Geological Survey; NOAA

A computer-generated image of Hurricane Fran, using information collected by a satellite. Hurricane Fran hit the country's east coast in 1989.

BLIZZARDS AND THUNDERSTORMS

Blizzards can occur in many areas, but are particularly common in the eastern states. In January 2001 all three of New York City's airports were closed by blizzards. There were also snowstorms much farther south. The southern state of Louisiana had 100mm of snow – its highest snowfall in 15 years. In Arkansas, ice storms linked to the blizzards cut electricity supplies to thousands of homes for nine days.

In central areas of the United States, cold, dense air travelling from the north meets

warm, moist air travelling up from the Gulf of Mexico, creating several climatic hazards. The warm, moist air is lifted up quite violently as the cold, denser air undercuts it. As it rises, the moist air condenses and forms huge cumulonimbus clouds, creating thunderstorms and lightning. Hailstones are also common, formed when raindrops caught in the rapidly rising air freeze and fall. Some hailstones are the size of as golf balls and can completely flatten large areas of crops.

TORNADOES

Tornadoes are caused by similar conditions to those that cause thunderstorms, but with the addition of a fast-moving upper air stream. The upper air stream turns the warm rising air and a revolving funnel is created. At ground level this tornado (or "twister") destroys everything in its path. Tornadoes can be up to a kilometer wide, but are usually less than 100m wide, with winds of up to 500km per hour. Tornado Alley is the name given to an area over Texas, Oklahoma, Kansas and Nebraska, where most of the large destructive tornadoes occur (see map on page 17). In April 2001 six people were killed by tornadoes in Mississippi and Arkansas, on the edge of Tornado Alley, and over 300 homes were damaged.

Abandoned cars in Buffalo, New York, after an unexpected snowstorm in November 2000.

CASE STUDY
HURRICANE FLOYD, SEPTEMBER 1999

In September 1999 Hurricane Floyd formed in the Mid-Atlantic, off the east coast of the United States. At first, observers predicted it would come ashore in Florida, and an evacuation of 2 million coastal residents was organized, the largest evacuation in the nation's history. However, Hurricane Floyd bypassed Florida and on 16 September came ashore in North Carolina instead. Although winds with speeds up to 160km per hour caused considerable damage, it was the torrential rain that caused most of the

problems. Over 500mm of rain fell in just 12 hours. After the worst of the hurricane had passed, the rivers rose rapidly and caused considerable flooding. The majority of the 35 deaths in North Carolina were due to drowning. Water supplies in the area were contaminated by waste from farms and damaged sewers, as well as by the carcasses of thousands of drowned pigs and chickens. Thousands of people were made homeless and the estimated cost of the damage was $6 billion. Once it came over the land Hurricane Floyd soon weakened, although heavy rains and gale-force winds occurred in much of the northeast.

In an old forest in the Cascade Mountains of Washington, logging machinery moves harvested logs.

RAW MATERIALS

The United States is rich in natural resources and is one of the world's top producers of minerals such as aluminum, copper and lead. There are also large deposits of coal, natural gas, petroleum and uranium. Most of the metals, including copper, are mined in the western states. The country produces 20 percent of the world's sulphur, most of which comes from the coastal areas of Louisiana and Texas.

Although the United States produces large amounts of minerals, it also imports several, such as zinc and silver, because it cannot produce enough to meet its own demand. The metals and minerals are used in a wide range of manufacturing industries. Sulphur is used in the manufacture of sulphuric acid and zinc is used in batteries.

Just under one-third of the country is forested and, of this amount, two-thirds is used as a timber resource, where trees are logged and sold. Softwoods such as pine are found mainly in the western coastal states, with hardwoods such as oak located more in southern states such as Georgia and North Carolina. Although sawn timber is important in the building industry (most American houses are timber framed), most timber is used as pulp for paper manufacturing.

CASE STUDY
FORESTS OF THE PACIFIC NORTHWEST

The western states of Washington and Oregon are famous for their evergreen forests, which consist mainly of coniferous trees such as the Douglas fir. Over 80 percent of these forests have been felled for timber. Of the remaining areas, only 20 percent are protected. Since these are ancient forests and an increasingly rare habitat, they need further protection. But conflict exists between conservationists and the logging industry. The US government has forbidden any more felling of the older areas of forest to protect the northern spotted owl, whose habitat is this ancient forest. The government's ban has had a damaging impact on local economies. In one local county in Oregon, after the owl was declared an endangered species in 1990, its annual timber-industry income fell from $12.7 to $2.1 million. Overall it was estimated that 100,000 jobs were lost in the northwest as a result of protecting the owl and its habitat. Loggers put stickers on their cars reading, "If it's hooting, I'm shooting!"

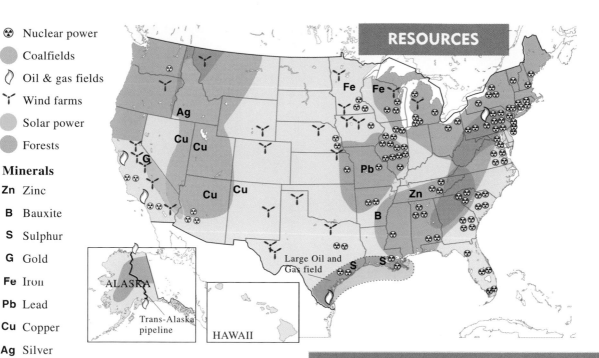

Legend:

- ☢ Nuclear power
- Coalfields
- Oil & gas fields
- Wind farms
- Solar power
- Forests

Minerals

- **Zn** Zinc
- **B** Bauxite
- **S** Sulphur
- **G** Gold
- **Fe** Iron
- **Pb** Lead
- **Cu** Copper
- **Ag** Silver

Fe Fe

Ag

Cu Cu

G

Pb

Cu Cu

Zn

B

Large Oil and Gas field

S S

ALASKA

Trans-Alaska pipeline

HAWAII

PRODUCTION OF METALS BY VALUE, 1999

Copper 27%

Iron 18%

Zinc 9%

Lead 5%

Silver 3%

Other 7%

Gold 31%

Source: US Census

CASE STUDY
COPPER MINING AT BINGHAM

The open-cast mine at Bingham Canyon.

Since 1998, copper production in the United States has diminished due to low world demand, and some mines in the country have had to close. The copper mine at Bingham Canyon, in Utah, is the largest human excavation in the world. Its huge size makes mining there profitable. The mine was modernized in the early 1990s to comply with new environmental laws, and a new smelter was built. Almost all (99.9 percent) of the sulphur produced in the smelting process is now captured by a new smelter. If the sulphur was allowed to escape it could form sulphur dioxide, which is a major ingredient in acid rain. The waste heat produced by the smelting process is recycled to generate power. Restoration work has been carried out on the old mine dumps and the mining company has won an environmental award for its care of the landscape. The mine has a workforce of over 2,000 people and pays total annual wages of $50 million. Property taxes paid by the mine help the local economy even more.

ENERGY

The United States uses 40 percent of the world's fossil fuel production. The average American family has a high standard of living that depends on fuel for at least two cars, heating in winter, and electricity to run air-conditioning in the summer and a large number of appliances in the home. This creates a huge demand for energy.

In April 2001 power cuts in California were caused by a drought in Washington state. Low flow in the rivers meant less hydroelectric power (HEP) was produced with no surplus to send to California. Many Americans began to look at alternative sources of energy.

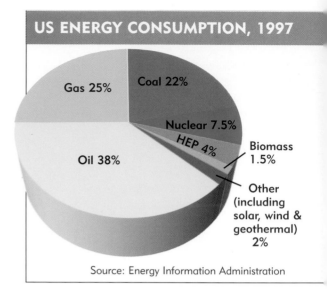

US ENERGY CONSUMPTION, 1997

Gas 25%
Coal 22%
Nuclear 7.5%
HEP 4%
Biomass 1.5%
Oil 38%
Other (including solar, wind & geothermal) 2%

Source: Energy Information Administration

COAL

The United States is the world's second-largest producer of coal after China. In 1999 there were about 1,800 coal mines in the east, the Rocky Mountains and the northern Great Plains. The leading coal-producing state is Wyoming, where the industry produces 26 percent of the nation's total output and employs nearly 5,000 people. The coal produced is low in sulphur and ash, so it burns more cleanly than coal from other areas. Most mining employs open-cast methods and

in some cases the coal is loaded automatically onto largest trains and sent directly to power stations. As coal is removed from the ground the landscape is restored, and grasses and trees are planted.

NUCLEAR POWER

In 2000, nuclear reactors produced 20 percent of the country's electricity. Amid concerns about its safety, no new nuclear power stations were planned. Between 2000 and 2001 the percentage of people in favor of nuclear power in the United States rose from 45 to 66

An open-cast coal mine in Gillette, Wyoming.

percent. Compared to coal-burning power stations, nuclear power is a cleaner type of fuel because it does not release carbon dioxide, which contributes toward global warming. Several new nuclear power stations are now planned.

However, one of the problems linked to nuclear power is the storage of radioactive waste. At Yucca Mountain, 140km north of Las Vegas, there is conflict between Native American communities and the nuclear power industry. The industry wants to create a huge underground nuclear dump beneath the mountain. The Native Americans are worried that the waste will contaminate water supplies. Since the waste will require 10,000 years to become safe, it presents a long-term problem.

RENEWABLE ENERGY

The United States has developed a wide range of renewable energy sources, including geothermal, wave, biomass, solar, wind and HEP. Solar power is becoming more popular in the warmer states, such as Florida and California. Solar "farms" in the desert areas of California use huge banks of solar cells to convert the sun's energy into power (see page 57). Since California's power cuts in April 2001, people have been paying to have solar panels put on their roofs in order to reduce their electricity bills and give them an alternative energy supply.

Biomass power includes landfill gas sites. It provides 1.5 percent of the country's energy. Timber waste is also used as a fuel for some

Large-scale wind farms, such as this one in California, provide Americans with an alternative power source to fossil fuels.

power stations.

Hydroelectric power is important on many of the country's rivers. The largest HEP plant is at the Grand Coulee Dam on the Columbia River, in Washington State. Usually, 75 percent of the electricity produced is sold outside the state, unless drought reduces production.

Wind energy in California provides 95 percent of the country's total wind power, yet this is only 1.5 percent of the state's total power needs. This amount represents 30 percent of the world's total wind energy production. New, large-scale wind farms across California use massive wind turbines to produce electricity.

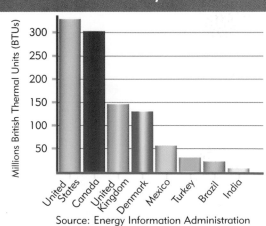

AVERAGE ENERGY CONSUMPTION PER PERSON, 1996

Millions British Thermal Units (BTUs)

300
250
200
150
100
50

United States, Canada, United Kingdom, Denmark, Mexico, Turkey, Brazil, India

Source: Energy Information Administration

OIL AND GAS

The United States has the twelfth-largest oil reserves in the world, producing 5.8 million barrels a day, plus large amounts of natural gas. Yet only 43 percent of the country's needs are met by its own oil wells; the rest has to be imported because the nation consumes 26 percent of the world's available oil. It is estimated that by 2025, the country's population will be greater than 300 million and only 15 per cent of its own oil will remain untapped.

The United States depends heavily on oil for transportation and industry. Its size and its limited public transport means there are not many alternatives to the car. At present, Americans pay less for their petrol than Europeans, and the government is reluctant to increase the price. But low prices are making it difficult for oil companies to survive, and many companies are merging so they can afford to explore and develop new oil fields.

The government has an emergency stockpile of 570 million barrels of oil stored in caverns along the Gulf of Mexico coast. In September 2000, some was released to cover a possible shortage of heating fuel for the winter.

The majority of oil is found within four states: Texas, Alaska, California and Louisiana.

TEXAS

The state of Texas produces 18 percent of the country's oil, and still maintains large reserves. Production peaked in 1972, but since then, even with new discoveries, it is continuing to decline. Most of the new oil and gas wells are located in the Gulf of Mexico. New technology means that offshore wells can now be sunk in deep water to tap the reserves.

Pipes raised above the snow carry oil to a collection centre in Alaska.

US PETROLEUM CONSUMPTION AND PRODUCTION, 1990–2000

Barrels per day (millions)

Consumption

Production

Source: Texas Petrofacts; Energy Information Administration

The Trans-Alaska oil pipeline at Prudhoe Bay, Alaska. The pipeline carries oil from the bay to the port at Valdez.

ALASKA

Alaska produces 17 percent of the country's oil, with most coming from the Prudhoe Bay field in north Alaska. Prudhoe Bay is a port, but it is covered in ice for much of the year, so the oil is warmed and pumped through a pipeline to the southern Alaskan port of Valdez. The pipeline is 1,280km long. It crosses three mountain ranges and nearly 800 rivers and streams before reaching Valdez, where oil is loaded onto tankers from the pipeline. For 672km, the pipeline is above ground because of the difficulties of burying it in frozen soil. The sections above ground follow a zig-zag path to allow the pipe to expand and contract, and to allow it to move during an earthquake. Some parts of the pipeline are over 3m above ground to allow herds of caribou to migrate underneath. Under rivers, the pipeline is insulated to prevent the warm oil from thawing the ground, which might then sink and allow oil to escape into the environment, damaging the fragile tundra vegetation.

OIL SPILL

One of the nation's worst oil spills occurred in 1989 when a tanker, the *Exxon Valdez*, ran aground near the port of Valdez, spilling 37,000 tonnes of oil. It caused an environmental disaster, covering much of the coastline in oil and killing fish, sea otters and other animals. Today the area has largely recovered, but it is still being monitored.

CASE STUDY
ARCTIC NATIONAL WILDLIFE REFUGE

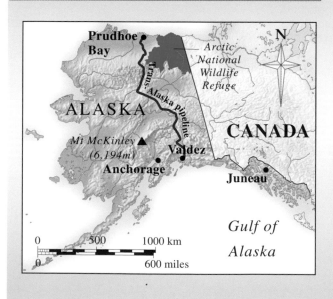

The Arctic National Wildlife Refuge is an area within Alaska that has, until now, been protected from oil exploration and development. Part of the refuge is thought to have oil deposits. If oil wells are dug in the area, only 10 percent of the reserve would be affected, but the oil-rich area includes most of the coastal plain, where caribou migrate and polar bears set up their breeding dens. In May 2001, President Bush said that the ANWR was to be opened up to oil exploration. The recovery of the oil will provide the United States with nine months' supply of its oil needs. Yet opponents to oil exploration claim that it could destroy an important wildlife refuge and interfere with the migration and breeding of the largest caribou herd on the continent.

PEOPLE OF THE UNITED STATES

The United States has a diverse population, the result of many migrations of people from different parts of the world. In 2000, its population was 280.6 million, having grown by 33 million since 1990. The population is a valuable resource to the country.

The original inhabitants of the country were Native Americans who migrated from Asia thousands of years ago. Today there are about 2 million Native Americans living in the United States, mostly in the west. Europeans arrived in America after Christopher Columbus landed in the West Indies in 1492, with settlement by the English, Spanish, Germans, French and Dutch. In the eighteenth century, black slaves were brought from Africa to the plantations of the southern states. In the nineteenth century, potato famines in Ireland triggered large migrations of Irish. Since then, there have been further waves of migration from China, southern and Eastern Europe, Latin America and Asia. Some immigrants came to America to escape religious persecution. Others came for the chance of a better life for themselves and for their children. Today, most immigrants are from Latin America, especially Mexico.

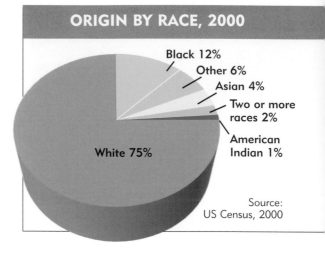

ORIGIN BY RACE, 2000

Black 12%
Other 6%
Asian 4%
Two or more races 2%
American Indian 1%
White 75%

Source: US Census, 2000

MEXICAN IMMIGRANTS

The United States shares a border with Mexico, and the high standard of living in the country acts as a magnet to Mexican immigrants. In 2000, the country's GDP per capita was $35,510 compared to only $5,500 in Mexico. There are few jobs in Mexico and nearly 40 percent of its population is unemployed.

In the United States, Mexicans have traditionally been employed as seasonal agricultural workers in states such as California, where they help with planting and harvesting. Many have stayed on and become legal US citizens. In 2000 there were 21 million Mexicans living in the country, forming nearly 8 percent of the population. California

A recent immigrant from Mexico at work in a clothing factory in El Paso, Texas.

These teenagers are performing a Mexican dance at a street festival in Austin, Texas.

has nearly 4 million legal Mexican residents, but this number is almost identical to the number of illegal immigrants. The Mexican border is patrolled by guards to stop the entry of illegal immigrants. Along isolated stretches of the Rio Grande River, on the Texas-Mexico boundary, many Mexicans try to swim across. They want decent jobs, access to health care and to be able to provide their children with a good education. To do this, they are willing to work in low-paid jobs that are often difficult to persuade American citizens to take.

At first, Mexican immigrants were concentrated in the southern states such as California and Texas, which have borders with Mexico. In 2000, Spanish speakers outnumbered English speakers in California. Mexicans are now moving to other parts of the United States, where there is less competition for jobs. Some are even moving to Alaska to work on fishing fleets.

Mexican influence can be seen on the streets of most cities in the United States.

There are Spanish-style fiestas, food shops and restaurants, as well as Spanish-language television and radio. New immigrants generally want to become Americans yet hold onto their language and culture.

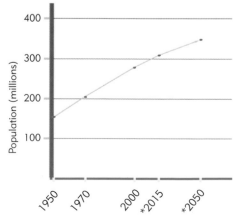

US POPULATION, 1950–2050

Population (millions)

400
300
200
100

1950 1970 2000 *2015 *2050

Sources: UN Population Division; Geographical Digest; UNDP. *= Estimates

AGRICULTURE, INDUSTRY AND TRADE

Wheat being harvested by giant combine harvesters in the northern Great Plains.

The United States is a world leader in agricultural production. In the east there is enough rainfall to support a range of crops and livestock. The soils are generally more fertile than farther west. Most corn (maize) is produced between the states of Ohio and Nebraska, and between Minnesota and Missouri. A belt of cotton production stretches from South Carolina to Texas.

In the interior of the country the climate is drier and there are vast expanses of wheat production. Extensive livestock rearing is found in the mountainous and very dry areas of the west, the land of the cowboy and cattle herding. Much of the west coast is a mixture of forests, crops and some livestock farming. Market gardening, a form of intensive agriculture with very high inputs of labor and chemicals, is found close to areas of large population, such as San Francisco and Los Angeles.

Farming employs only about 2 percent of the country's working population. Over the last 50 years, farms have become fewer in number but much larger in size. This is because it is cheaper to run a larger farm, since chemicals, feedstuffs and fuel can be purchased at a discount in large quantities. Farming large fields also reduces labor costs.

ECONOMIC STRUCTURE, 1999 (% GDP CONTRIBUTION)

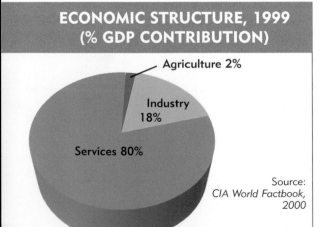

Agriculture 2%

Industry 18%

Services 80%

Source: CIA World Factbook, 2000

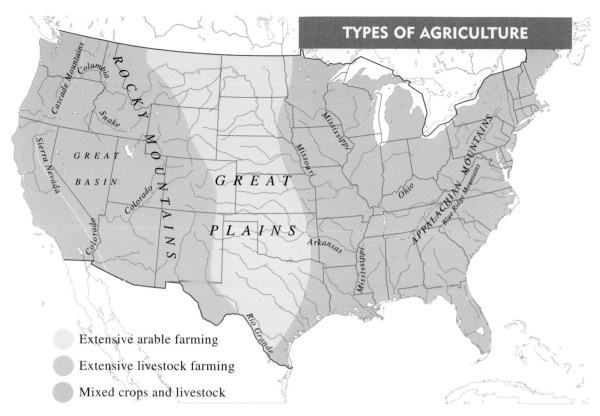

ROCKY MOUNTAINS

Cascade Mountains

Columbia

Snake

Sierra Nevada

GREAT BASIN

Colorado

Colorado

GREAT PLAINS

Missouri

Mississippi

Arkansas

Mississippi

Ohio

APPALACHIAN MOUNTAINS

Blue Ridge Mountains

Rio Grande

- Extensive arable farming
- Extensive livestock farming
- Mixed crops and livestock

CASE STUDY
IRRIGATED FARMING IN THE COLUMBIA BASIN

Vineyards in Washington State. The United States is one of the world's leading producers of wine.

Although western Washington has high rainfall, once inland, under the rain shadow of the Rocky Mountains, rainfall is very low. Irrigation from the Columbia River and its tributaries has made this region into a highly productive area. Washington State is the country's leading producer of apples, growing 6 billion per year and 33 percent of the entire US crop. In the valley of the Yakima River, a tributary of the Columbia, the soil and temperatures are ideal for growing apples and many other fruits. Water is taken from the Yakima to irrigate the crops, achieving high levels of production. All of the nation's hops (for use in beer making) are grown under irrigation in the Yakima Valley, making the country the second-largest producer of beer in the world. The world's largest-producing area of spearmint is on the Columbia Plateau. Irrigated farming is an intensive type of agriculture because of the high costs involved, particularly that of transporting water. Although increasingly mechanized, many of the crops still demand a large amount of labor.

A steelworks in Pittsburgh, Pennsylvania, being demolished piece by piece in 1983.

THE RUST BELT

Manufacturing first began in the United States near the Atlantic ports, but as the population moved westward it developed in the new cities along the Great Lakes and along the navigable rivers of the region (see map on page 31). At the beginning of the twentieth century a manufacturing belt stretched from Chicago in the west to Boston, New York and Baltimore in the east. It was the most important manufacturing region in the world, especially for steel. This manufacturing belt developed and expanded because of the locally available raw materials, especially iron ore and coal, and the good transportation links by water, rail and later by road. There was also access to the large markets in the east of the region.

In the second half of the twentieth century, many of the older, heavy industries in the region, such as steelmaking, declined. This was partially due to competition from overseas, but also due to world overproduction of steel, which drove down its price. The region was renamed the "rust belt."

PITTSBURGH

Pittsburgh was perhaps the city most strongly linked to the steel industry. Its rivers carried in iron ore and coal, which were used to make steel. The same rivers were used to take away the finished product. By 1983 the city's economy was in decline, and 80,000 steelmaking jobs had been lost over the previous year. However, the wealth created in the past had founded several good colleges and universities, which helped drive industrial change through the city.

Since the 1980s, many hi-tech firms have been attracted to Pittsburgh by tax incentives, and by the ability to access research and development carried out in the universities. Pittsburgh is now the fifth-largest producer of software in the United States. The loss of heavy industry has led to cleaner air and a more pleasant environment. The old steel

plants along the rivers have been converted into warehouses or small business units. The city now has a more varied industrial base.

DETROIT

The city of Detroit was known as "Motown" (motor town) because car manufacture used to be its main industry. Again, because of foreign competition, this industry has been in decline and there have been many job losses. But a $100-billion-scheme has been started to regenerate the economy and to attract new businesses. Some of the new firms are eager to use the city's highly skilled workforce. The former Cadillac assembly plant is being developed as a technology park and should create as many as 1,700 permanent jobs when it is completed.

CHICAGO

Chicago is the main city in the rust belt. It grew because of its position on Lake Michigan, and later as the hub of many railway routes. A canal links the lake to the Mississippi River, giving access to the south of the United States. Chicago's traditional industries include meat processing and steelmaking. In the recession of the 1980s, most of the city's steel industries closed down, but Chicago already had a wider industrial base than most cities. It is an

important financial and banking center, and is the site of many company headquarters. In April 2001 the airplane company Boeing decided to move its headquarters to Chicago from Seattle, largely because of its central location.

The cities of the rust belt continue to face challenges. During the early months of 2001 there were further losses in manufacturing. But the cities are fighting to develop a more varied industrial base, and to move into the twenty-first century with a more stable, multi-industry economy.

Traders work frantically inside Chicago's giant Stock Exchange.

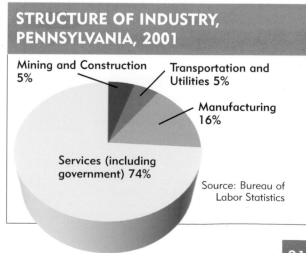

THE SUNBELT – BOOM OR BUST?

The Sunbelt area originally included two states, Florida and California, but it now includes other states, such as Georgia, Tennessee and Alabama, and its definitions are constantly changing. These states all have a warm, sunny climate, which attracts residents and workers. The industries that have grown in these locations are mainly hi-tech, not tied to the sources of raw materials. They include computer development and the production of semiconductors. These industries are known as "footloose industries" and are typical of the late twentieth and early twenty-first centuries. Since they are market-oriented, they are located near large centers of population where their products are sold, or close to transport routes that offer easy access to such centers.

Hi-tech industries tend to be located near

The headquarters of a large computer firm in Silicon Valley, California.

Inset: Jobs in hi-tech industries are sought after because they are usually well paid.

universities, so they can have access to research. Flat land is required for landscaped company factories, with room for expansion. The industries generally create very little noise or pollution, and can be built near residential areas. They are usually close to airports, so it is easy to import component parts and export the finished goods.

SILICON VALLEY, CALIFORNIA

The area known as Silicon Valley lies just south of San Francisco. It is the main area within the United States for the design and production of microchips, electronic circuitry and computer software. Large numbers of firms are located here around Stanford University. In the 1950s

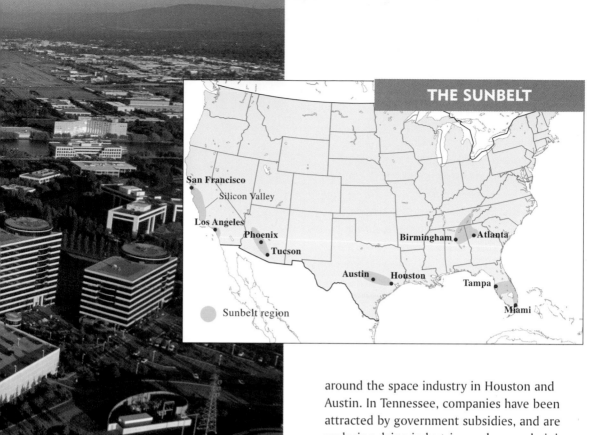

San Francisco
Silicon Valley
Los Angeles
Phoenix
Tucson
Birmingham
Atlanta
Austin
Houston
Tampa
Miami

Sunbelt region

the university leased some land to hi-tech companies to help raise money for expansion. Over the years more companies arrived, attracted by the university, good road routes, nearby airports, and the pleasant climate for their employees. Employees stay in each job for an average of two years in the Silicon Valley, and it is common for people to move to rival firms, or to set up their own. All employees are encouraged to think of ideas for new products in order to keep their company ahead of the rest of the world in new technology.

LOS ANGELES, TEXAS AND TENNESSEE

Other hi-tech areas within the Sunbelt are found in Los Angeles. Here, the government's investment in the aerospace industry over the past 50 years has created large numbers of firms that produce components. Other groups of hi-tech companies are found in Texas, based around the space industry in Houston and Austin. In Tennessee, companies have been attracted by government subsidies, and are replacing dying industries such as coalmining.

BUST

At the beginning of 2001, many employees in the computer industry lost their jobs as a number of computer businesses failed due to the worldwide overproduction of microchips. The hi-tech industries had grown too fast. The industry is necessary to all sectors of the economy, but future growth must now be steady and carefully financed.

STRUCTURE OF INDUSTRY, CALIFORNIA, 2001

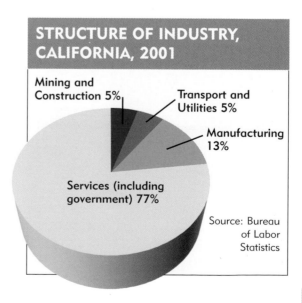

Mining and Construction 5%
Transport and Utilities 5%
Manufacturing 13%
Services (including government) 77%

Source: Bureau of Labor Statistics

APPALACHIA – THE "BYPASSED AREA"

Appalachia is the name of a region that covers the southern Appalachian Mountains, and includes parts of eight states. It is a poor region, made up of highlands that include the Blue Ridge and Great Smoky Mountains. These mountains were a barrier to early settlement. In the early nineteenth century, Scots, Irish, English and German settlers built small farms in the narrow river valleys. Since then there has been very little movement into or out of the region. Appalachian society is based on the family, and the local church plays an important role, often providing the social center for a settlement.

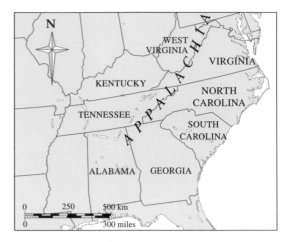

AGRICULTURE

Farms in the narrow valleys are small (about 40 hectares) and the climate can be harsh. The soils are often poor, except in the valley bottoms, and the fields are small, so it is not easy to use agricultural machinery. The farms are semi-marginal, which means they can only just support a family. Crops such as tobacco and apples are sold, but production levels are low. Appalachian farms cannot compete with more commercial farming areas such as the Great Plains.

MINING

Huge deposits of coal lie under the plateau section of Appalachia. Until the 1980s it was used to make coke for the country's iron and steel industries, and to generate power. Its use declined in the 1980s and 1990s because Appalachian coal has a high sulphur content. The government's emission laws became stricter, so other less polluting forms of coal are now used in most power stations. The government has recently helped put new sulphur-removing technology into Appalachia's power stations, so that local coal continues to be used. A third of the mining is done using open-cast methods, which has a major impact on the landscape. Ten years ago there were 48 mining companies in the region. Today there are only eight, and their future is not certain. Mechanization has reduced the number of miners needed to work the remaining pits. Most of the profits leave the region because the companies that own the mines are based elsewhere.

GOVERNMENT HELP

The government has set up a series of initiatives to try to improve the quality of life in Appalachia. Empowerment Zones have been created to encourage private investment with

In the winter, Appalachian towns in the mountains can become isolated.

tax incentives and help with building costs. New interstate highways were built during the 1990s to reduce Appalachia's isolation and to encourage businesses to move to the region. The Federal Bureau of Investigation (FBI) moved its fingerprinting facility into Appalachia, creating 2,600 local jobs. There is a small cluster of more than 70 hi-tech firms providing 1,000 jobs in the same area. Apart from these, most new jobs are in the low-wage sectors of service industries.

EDUCATION

The population of Appalachia is aging, as younger people leave the region for better prospects. The percentage of students receiving high school diplomas is now higher than the national average. Young people view a diploma as a ticket out of the area, or as entry into the higher-paid, skilled jobs within the region.

TOURISM

Tourism is becoming increasingly important in Appalachia, especially in areas away from the new interstate highways. Tourists are attracted by the region's beautiful scenery and autumnal forest colors, which rival those of New England. The number of second homes being purchased in the region has increased, as middle-class families in Atlanta buy cabins in the Blue Ridge Mountains for the weekends.

Appalachia still has many problems, including relatively low incomes, but its industrial base is becoming more varied and its population is now generally healthier and better educated. The "bypassed area" has begun to join the rest of the country.

APPALACHIA: STANDARD OF LIVING

	Appalachia	United States
Income per capita, 1999	$24,871	$28,518
Rural dwellers	44%	20%
Unemployed	4.6%	4.5%
Infant mortality per 1,000	8.3	8
Telephone owners	80%	95%

Source: US Census; Appalachian Regional Commission

Guitar and banjo players playing on the porch of the Appalachian Museum during the Tennessee Fall Homecoming Festival.

WORLD TRADE AND AID

The United States is a wealthy and influential nation. It carries out a large amount of trade with the rest of the world, including non- democratic countries such as China. Yet its balance of trade is in the red; it imports far more than it exports, and has a trading debt of $32 billion. The trading deficit is particularly bad with Japan ($6.2 billion). The country's top exports include military equipment, cereals, processed foods, cars and machinery. In March 2001

This worker at a factory in South Korea is making goods for the US company Nike.

total imports were worth $120 billion. Total exports were worth $88 billion.

AMERICAN EXPORTS

Other important American exports are from its music, film and television industries. Disney animations and major film blockbusters are sold and seen worldwide. The United States is the home of rock music, the blues and rap, and

MAJOR TRADING PARTNERS (% GDP), 1998

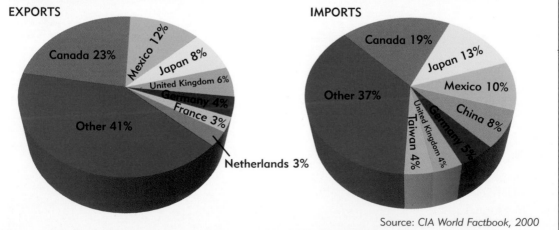

EXPORTS

Canada 23%
Mexico 12%
Japan 8%
United Kingdom 6%
Germany 4%
France 3%
Other 41%
Netherlands 3%

IMPORTS

Canada 19%
Japan 13%
Mexico 10%
China 8%
Germany 5%
United Kingdom 4%
Taiwan 4%
Other 37%

Source: CIA World Factbook, 2000

GDP PER CAPITA

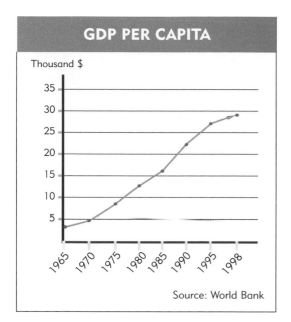

Thousand $

Source: World Bank

there is a constant flow of pop music sold around the world. Large numbers of American television programs, especially soap operas and chat shows, are exported, and have become an integral part of the culture of many countries, including the United Kingdom and Canada.

Major American food chains are located in towns and cities in all corners of the world. American clothing and footwear have a powerful influence because of their branding. Certain logos are recognized over much of the developed world and many people will pay a high price for them. However, many products with a US brand are not actually made in the United States. Instead they are made in countries such as Vietnam, South Korea or the Philippines, where the wages are much lower.

NATO AND THE UN

The United States is a member of many powerful world organizations, including the North Atlantic Treaty Organization (NATO). NATO is a defense alliance consisting of the United States and 15 other countries. It was set up in 1949 to counter the influence of the communist Soviet Union. Since the end of the Cold War, former communist and socialist countries, such as Russia, have also had a

voice within NATO.

The country is also a member of the United Nations (UN), a group set up after the Second World War, which protects human rights and the environment, and attempts to eradicate poverty in the world. The UN also has a peacekeeping role, providing troops and observers in areas of conflict, such as Bosnia and Sierra Leone. The contribution of the United States to the UN's peacekeeping funds has been calculated at 30 percent. However, the nation believes it should only contribute 25 percent. This is affecting the UN's ability to carry out its role in times of crisis.

AID

The United States provides funds for the development of poorer nations. This includes projects to improve agriculture, to increase childhood immunization against diseases, to combat HIV and AIDS, and to improve the level of female literacy. However, although the United States does contribute a great deal of money to overseas aid, the amount represents a tiny percentage of its Gross Domestic Product. The UN recommends that developed nations donate 0.7 percent of their GDP to aid. At present the US contribution is only 0.09 percent.

US troops taking part in the Gulf War against Iraq, in 1991.

TRANSPORT AND URBANIZATION

A freight train makes its way across the American Midwest.

GETTING AROUND

The United States is a country of huge distances. To drive from New York in the northeast, to Los Angeles in the southwest is a journey of more than 4,000km. Transport is a major sector of the country's economy and contributes $980 billion per year to the Gross Domestic Product. The industry transports raw materials and finished products as well as passengers, and it also employs large numbers of people.

RAIL

The railways originally opened up the west of the country to settlement, but today they are not the most important form of transport. The railway network is most dense on the eastern side of the country. Only a few passenger lines cross the country. In California, more railway lines are being developed, and buses are linking areas that do not have access to a railway. This is to encourage people to leave the heavily congested roads. Between Boston and Washington, D.C., a high-speed rail service called the Acela Express increased its use by 10 percent in 2001. The train travels at up to 240km per hour and offers a fast alternative to flying or going by road.

The railways are still important for transporting long-distance, heavy freight, such as coal, iron ore and timber products. The Union Pacific Railroad is one of the largest freight carriers and serves the 23 western states. It links every major West Coast and Gulf Coast port. Many freight trains carry large amounts of a single type of freight, which keeps costs down. The amount of rail freight is increasing because the fuel costs of moving large quantities can be much lower than transporting by road.

AIR TRAVEL

For travel within the United States, many people choose to fly rather than go by road. There are over 5,000 airports in the country. In 1999 the busiest airport was in Atlanta, Georgia, a gateway airport to other flight journeys, which counted 37 million passengers.

WATER TRANSPORT

Water transport is important for carrying goods. The Great Lakes link the industrial

Passengers in the terminal building at Austin-Bergstrom International Airport in Austin, Texas.

and 8 million trucks. The country has a system of interstate highways, with wide, well-maintained roads between major cities and across the country. They are used by the trucking industry and carry a great deal of freight. For much of the country there is no alternative to the car because very few places have access to a railway. Public transport systems such as the New York Subway are only well developed in areas with a high population density. At present, only 5 percent of the US population uses public transport.

Problems with such a heavy dependency on the car include poor air quality, heavy traffic congestion and a rapidly decreasing oil supply. Car journey times are increasing, but are still shorter than the average time taken when using public transport.

cities on their shores to the Atlantic Ocean, and ocean-going vessels can move between them. The nation has many important ports, the most important being South Louisiana, at the mouth of the Mississippi. The port deals with 4,000 ocean-going ships and 5,000 river barges per year. It links the Gulf of Mexico to the inland barge system via the Mississippi, and gives access to 31,000km of inland waterway.

ROAD TRANSPORT

The majority of transport in the United States is by road. There are nearly 132 million cars

The United States must find alternatives to such a heavy dependence on the car as an individual form of transportation. One suggestion is the use of fully automated highway systems that are currently being tested in Japan. Here, groups of cars are computer-controlled on the motorways so that more traffic can be carried at any one time. The control systems monitor accelerating, braking, and distances between vehicles. They may provide a solution to the congested freeways of cities like Los Angeles.

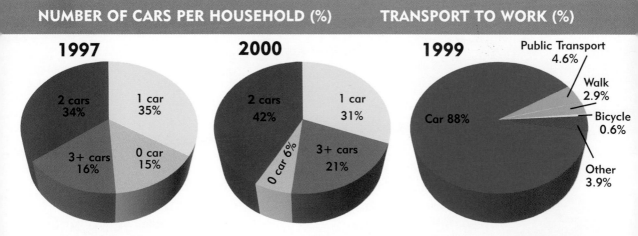

NUMBER OF CARS PER HOUSEHOLD (%)

1997
- 2 cars 34%
- 1 car 35%
- 3+ cars 16%
- 0 car 15%

2000
- 2 cars 42%
- 1 car 31%
- 0 car 6%
- 3+ cars 21%

TRANSPORT TO WORK (%)

1999
- Car 88%
- Public Transport 4.6%
- Walk 2.9%
- Bicycle 0.6%
- Other 3.9%

Sources: US Census; Bureau of Transportation Statistics; Nationwide Personal Transport Survey

URBANIZATION

The United States is now a largely urban country, with 75 percent of the population living in towns and cities. The fastest urban growth is mainly in the south and west of the country.

The nation's earliest settlements were established along the Atlantic coast by European settlers in the seventeenth century. The coastal plain was fairly flat, which made settlement easy. Ships brought manufactured goods to the ports and took away furs, timber and crops. Some sites, such as Boston and New York, also had the advantage of being at the mouths of rivers. This helped send goods via the rivers farther inland, where other towns developed.

Throughout the eighteenth and nineteenth centuries these eastern cities continued to grow, as industries developed based on goods flowing through their ports. In the nineteenth century, railways made links between cities much faster than by water. Some cities, such as Chicago, grew because they were situated where several railway lines converged.

BOSTON AND THE EAST

In the twentieth century, five cities continued to grow in the east: Boston, New York, Philadelphia, Baltimore and Washington, D.C. These five large urban areas merged to form an extensive, largely urbanized landscape, stretching from Boston down to Washington, D.C. Called Boswash, it is a megalopolis.

EARLY IMMIGRATION

Boston was settled by early immigrants from England in 1630. The site was mainly flat, with low hills at the center. There was a good water supply and easy access to water transport. Boston's early wealth came from trade with Europe. Banks and financial institutions were set up to support the trade. Processing industries such as flour milling flourished. At the end of the nineteenth century a wide range of manufacturing was carried out, including textiles

Manhattan Island, New York City, is surrounded by four rivers, including the East River on its eastern border and the Hudson on its west. This photo was taken before 11 September 2001, when the Twin Towers of the World Trade Center (on the left of the picture) were destroyed by terrorists.

and shipbuilding. Several waves of immigrants came to Boston to work in the expanding industries, including Italians, who arrived beginning 1870. Italian culture still dominates several areas of the city.

INDUSTRIAL CHANGE

The twentieth century saw the decline of many of Boston's traditional industries, although clothing and leather industries still remain. Most goods are now transported by road or rail, or shipped out through the port of New York City. Boston is still important as a financial and academic center, and it has seen the rise of hi-tech industries, clustered along Route 128. One of the main reasons for their location in Boston is that the city is linked to Harvard University and the Massachusetts Institute of Technology (MIT).

Tourism is becoming increasingly important for the city because of its many ties to the nation's early history. Parts of central Boston, such as Beacon Hill, look more European than American, with their narrow, cobbled streets and small houses.

CONGESTION

One of Boston's problems is traffic congestion. The main six-lane elevated highway through the city is jammed for at least seven hours each day. A project is underway, called "The Big Dig," which involves building an underground, eight-lane expressway to replace the elevated highway. Tunnels will also be built, to give Boston new links with its airport. The Big Dig is due to be completed in 2004 and will improve central Boston's landscape and air quality. It will also create 60 hectares of open space and parks.

Boston's population is still growing, its hi-tech industries continue to develop and it is attracting more young professionals to live and work there. Older areas of the city have been redeveloped to improve conditions, with many attractive waterfront locations. The city is still important for banking and finance, which, along with hi-tech industries, tourism and the remaining traditional industries, give Boston a sound foundation for the future.

The entrance to one of the huge road tunnels that are being built as part of "The Big Dig" in Boston, Massachusetts.

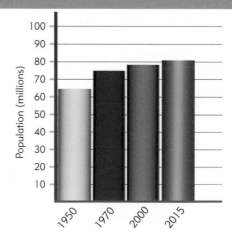

URBAN POPULATION GROWTH, 1950–2015

Source: *Geographical Digest;* UNDP

The urban sprawl of Los Angeles covers a vast area, linked together by freeways.

LOS ANGELES, LAS VEGAS AND THE NEW URBANIZATION

Los Angeles grew massively in the twentieth century, with a population reaching 3.5 million by 2000. It became the nation's second-largest city after New York. Its original growth was based on agriculture, particularly citrus groves. Later growth was due to the development of its oil, film and aerospace industries. Today, the city continues to attract people with its climate and lifestyle. Its low-density suburbs have spread out into the desert, earning Los Angeles the name of "Sixty-Mile City."

LAS VEGAS

The country's fastest-growing city is Las Vegas, the gambling capital of the world. In 1990 its population was 470,000. By 2000 it had grown to 1.4 million. The city was founded in 1904 with the development of the railway. It made an ideal stopping point in the desert because of the springs found there.

The first hotels were constructed in the 1940s. Today there are huge casino hotels offering a wide range of shows and entertainment, as well as constant access to gaming tables and slot machines.

Las Vegas attracts huge numbers of tourists all year round. An increasing number of people, attracted by the bright lights, the dry desert atmosphere and the nonexistent state income tax, want to move to the city permanently. Every year 60,000 people move to Las Vegas.

PROBLEMS OF GROWTH

The growth of Las Vegas has caused problems. The city suffers from air pollution due to the increasingly heavy traffic flows, and traffic jams are common at all times of the day. There is not enough water for the growing population and, as water is extracted from aquifers beneath the city, the land is sinking.

More suburbs are being built out in the desert, placing increased stress on the water supplies, roads, schools and other services of the city. The citizens of Las Vegas are deciding whether their city should be allowed to continue to grow at its present rate.

GATED COMMUNITIES

At the end of the twentieth century, urban developments called gated communities were established. Several can be found in Florida. Houses are purchased within a community, where the only access is via a barrier manned by a guard. The entire complex is walled. Often, these communities are dominated by senior citizens who are worried about crime and feel secure within this type of development.

The main street of Las Vegas, the gambling capital of the United States and the world.

As America continues to urbanize, problems such as crime rates, traffic congestion and poor air quality have been carried into the twenty-first century. Future growth of cities is being questioned and alternatives to growth are being researched.

CASE STUDY
CELEBRATION, FLORIDA

One of the streets in Celebration, a town built by the Disney Corporation.

Celebration, in Florida, is a new town that has been planned and developed by the Walt Disney Company. It is not a theme park but a real community based on what a small town would have been like in America 50 years ago. It is not gated, but people who live in Celebration must abide by certain rules. Only certain colors can be used to paint the fronts of houses. Shrubs in gardens must not be too large. Already, the early residents feel that the community is taking shape. There is a school, a bank, shops and a hospital. Residents have the use of electric vehicles to get around the town, which are less polluting than petrol-driven motors. All amenities are designed to be within walking distance of individual homes. The crime rate is very low and residents say that this is a reflection of the community spirit found in the town.

PEOPLE AND CULTURE

High school students of Asian, African and European origins studying together.

THE AMERICAN FAMILY

Although there are areas of great poverty within the United States, the average standard of living is high. About 99 percent of households have a television and 55 percent of children have a television in their bedrooms. Americans watch an average of five hours of television per day. Families eat out frequently, and there are many chains of restaurants that offer reasonably priced family meals. Most teenagers expect to learn to drive at the age of 16, and hope to have their own car.

AVERAGE AMERICAN FAMILY

Average household size with children	3.9
Infant mortality per 1,000 births	8
Life expectancy	76 years
Average annual family income before tax	$45,476
Age of consent	16
Age able to obtain a driving licence	16
Average number of TVs per household	2.1
Average number of cars per household	2.0

Source: US Census; American Factfinder; Consumer Expenditure Survey

TYPICAL AMERICAN HOUSES

Most children are raised in the suburbs. The average family house has three to four bedrooms with at least two bathrooms, and several telephones and televisions. The refridgerators are large because food shopping is not done every day, so items need to be stored. Food is bought in large supermarkets in shopping complexes within the suburb. Most suburban houses feature a lawn at the front and an enclosed garden in the back.

SCHOOL

In a typical American family, both parents are likely to work outside the home, driving their cars to work. Children go to a nursery, or kindergarten, from an early age while their parents are at work. Nursery costs are high and use up much of one of the two household incomes. Schooling is free and funded by each state. There are 12 grades, which students attend from the ages of six to 18. Elementary school covers Grades 1 to 5 and Junior High covers Grades 6 to 8. Then, students move to Senior High for the last four years. Students can leave school at 16, but few do since it is difficult to get a decent job without having completed high school. At 18 years old, students are awarded their high school diplomas and graduate from school with a formal ceremony.

COLLEGE

After high school many students study for a degree, for which they are expected to study a range of subjects. Some attend their local college, where the fees are cheaper and they can live at home. After two years, students are awarded an Associate Degree. If they continue for an additional two years, they will earn a BA or BS degree. Private universities such as Harvard, Yale and Princeton are members of the "Ivy League," comprising the top universities in the nation.

FIRST JOB AND MARRIAGE

The first job for American graduates often involves moving to a city, where they might share an apartment with other graduates. Their jobs will give them an average of two weeks vacation per year.

LIFE EXPECTANCY AT BIRTH

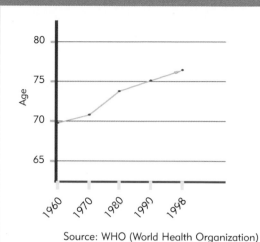

Source: WHO (World Health Organization)

Marriage is declining in the United States, but more couples are living together. The average age for marriage is about 26 years old. Many families look for a house in the suburbs because of the lower crime rate and the community feel.

HEALTH AND THE ELDERLY

There is no nationwide social service in the United States, and very limited welfare provision. Families are expected to save or to pay for insurance to cover themselves during old age or illness.

Many elderly people move to states such as Florida, where the weather is pleasant all year round. Sometimes older people live in housing estates with residents of a similar age, where there is a high level of security provision. Others choose to live in small houses or apartments near their families. There is a wide range of activities and societies designed especially for the elderly. The over-65s is a powerful group in the country because of its increasing numbers. By 2025, 20 percent of the population will be over 65 years old and will want to have more of a say in how American society is run.

UNDER-FIVE MORTALITY RATE

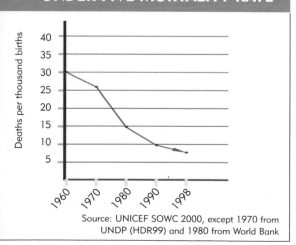

Source: UNICEF SOWC 2000, except 1970 from UNDP (HDR99) and 1980 from World Bank

LEISURE

Americans generally work longer hours than Europeans, and spend an average of eight hours a week travelling to and from work. This means the time available for leisure activities is on average only 20 hours a week. Employers often demand that their employees take their two weeks of vacation separately, so that their work is not disrupted. Americans must carefully plan their limited leisure time.

Reading is the most popular leisure activity, and 62 percent of adult Americans buy a daily newspaper. There are over 3,000 newspapers published in the country; some have a national coverage, such as *USA Today*, *The Washington Post* and the *New York Times*. The others cover local or state news. There are about 10,000 magazines, some of which boast huge numbers of readers. The most popular magazine – *Modern Maturity* – is aimed at retired people and has a circulation of 21 million copies.

Television is popular with all family members, with several main channels plus many more local networks. The Public Broadcasting Service (PBS) is run by the government; it features documentaries, discussion programs and drama.

Most socializing is based around the family, although going out for a meal is an everyday event since it is relatively cheap. Barbecues are popular, with many houses having one built into their backyard. In warmer parts of

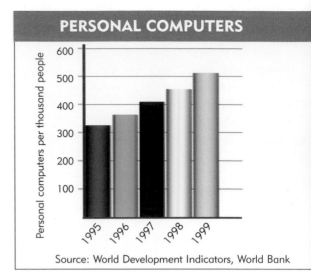

PERSONAL COMPUTERS

Source: World Development Indicators, World Bank

the United States, where swimming pools are common, pool parties are combined with the barbecue. Alcohol cannot be served to anyone under the age of 21. While city bars serve a range of customers, small-town bars tend to feature a loyal clientele.

SPORTS

Sports are popular as spectator activities but are also ones in which people take part. Baseball, basketball and football are favorites. Every county has a baseball league and each major city has a team that

Football is one of the country's favorite sports, alongside basketball and baseball.

competes at a national level. There are many amateur teams, as baseball games are family affairs.

Outdoor activities are also popular, with 42 percent of Americans taking part in at least one. Walking is a favorite activity, followed by swimming. National parks are the most popular outdoor destination, with 46 percent of Americans having visited at least one during the last 12 months.

CAMPING

Another favorite activity is weekend camping. Many families rent or own a Recreational Vehicle (RV), which is a large camper van, usually about 5 to 6 meters in length. They are well equipped with air-conditioning, a kitchen, bathroom and wardrobe space. RVs can often be seen on the road, towing a large car or four- wheel-drive vehicle, ready for use once the RV reaches a camping ground.

Camping is also popular for holidays. The United States is such a vast country that many families do not even leave their own state to go on vacation, and only about 20 percent of

A "recreational vehicle" (RV) winds its way through the Zion National Park in Utah.

the population travels abroad. The most popular destinations are Canada and Mexico, which border the country. If money were not a restriction, the most popular choice of destination would be Australia, followed closely by the United Kingdom.

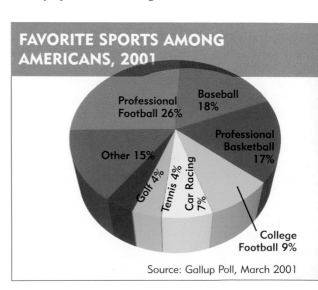

FAVORITE SPORTS AMONG AMERICANS, 2001

Professional Football 26%
Baseball 18%
Professional Basketball 17%
Other 15%
Golf 4%
Tennis 4%
Car Racing 7%
College Football 9%

Source: Gallup Poll, March 2001

TOURISM IN THE UNITED STATES

Tourism brings a great deal of money into the country. In 1999 foreign visitors spent nearly $70 billion, and almost 10 million jobs are dependent on the tourism industry. Worldwide, the United States is the third most-popular destination after France and Spain. In 1999, 47 million visitors travelled to the country.

Visitors to the United States have an enormous range of cities and landscapes from which to choose. They can visit specialist cities like Las Vegas, which is based on gambling, or New Orleans, where the French influence

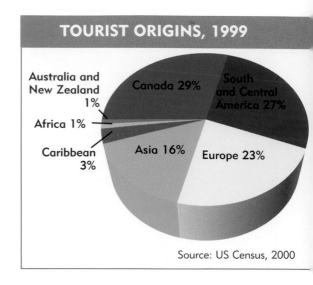

TOURIST ORIGINS, 1999

Australia and New Zealand 1%
Africa 1%
Caribbean 3%
Canada 29%
South and Central America 27%
Asia 16%
Europe 23%

Source: US Census, 2000

CASE STUDY
NEW YORK CITY

New York City is the most popular city destination for both foreign and domestic tourists. The "Big Apple," as it is known, is a huge city of more than 9 million people. Most of the sights of New York lie within Manhattan Island, including the famous Central Park. The city has many historical sights, including Ellis Island, where millions of immigrants entered the country. Most tourists visit the Statue of Liberty, which stands on Liberty Island and dominates New York Harbor.

There are many important museums in the city, such as the Museum of Modern Art (MOMA). Theatres are found in the district centered on Broadway. Carnegie Hall, an important venue for music, is also located

Tourists take photographs of the Statue of Liberty, from a boat in New York Harbor.

here. Major sporting events take place in Madison Square Garden.

New York City is multicultural, with many areas of the city reflecting the homelands of immigrants. Areas such as Chinatown, Little Ukraine and Little India preserve styles from different cultures.

remains. They can visit cultural centers, such as Boston, New York City and Atlanta.

Many visitors are attracted to the country's varied and diverse landscapes, from the desert areas of the southwest, through the rolling, grassy plains of the central states, the mountain scenery of the Rocky Mountains, the subtropical areas around Florida to the islands of Hawaii.

There are many opportunities for sports. The mountains in both the east and west are home to several major ski resorts. Watersports of all types can be undertaken along many of the coastal stretches and on the inland lakes. Some of these lakes, such as Lake Powell, are artificial. Lake Powell was created behind the Glen Canyon Dam on the Colorado River.

Florida is the most popular domestic destination for Americans. This state has excellent beaches combined with a variety of theme parks. Las Vegas remains a favorite among adult couples.

CASE STUDY
MONUMENT VALLEY

A Navajo woman weaves a traditional blanket for tourists, in Monument Valley.

Monument Valley is on the Arizona/Utah border. It is owned and managed by the Navajo, a group of Native Americans. There are about 400,000 visitors a year to this valley. It was named after its "monuments," sandstone spires and arches, and the remnants of volcanoes. These landforms are set in a sandy desert landscape, which has served as the backdrop for many cowboy films and numerous advertisements. Visitors can hire jeeps with Navajo drivers to take them around this spectacular and sacred land. As well as guiding tourists, the Navajo make and sell silver jewelry and Native American crafts.

Visitors explore the Everglades National Park, Florida, in an airboat.

NATIONAL PARKS

The country's national parks protect special or vulnerable landscapes, preserving their wildlife and history. They are also a valuable part of the tourist industry. The world's first national park was established in the United States in 1872, at Yellowstone in Wyoming. The aim of this first park was to protect the landscape and preserve it for future generations. Today, there are 54 national parks covering a wide range of landscapes, from the tundra and forests of Alaska to the desert and sandstone arches of Utah.

National parks are an important resource to Americans because they can be used for outdoor recreation, which provides an escape from the stresses of a mainly urban life. Toward the end of the twentieth century, their popularity resulted in increased pressures on the roads and amenities within some national parks, especially those within a few hours of large centers of population. Many parks experience problems with overcrowding at certain times of the year. Officials are now working on ways to attract tourists outside the busiest months, in order to even the flow of visitors.

CASE STUDY
THE GRAND CANYON NATIONAL PARK

The Grand Canyon National Park is perhaps the most spectacular national park in the country. It also has world importance and has been designated as a World Heritage Site. Located in northern Arizona, it consists of a deep, steep-walled canyon made up of many different layers of rock, with the Colorado River flowing at its base. The river flows more than 1.5km below the rim of the canyon. A descent of the canyon passes through four different vegetation zones. To encounter the same range one would need to travel from Canada to the state of New Mexico, a distance of nearly 2,000km! A former US president said of the Grand Canyon that it was "the one great sight every American... should see."

Most visitors come to the Grand Canyon's South Rim, which is open all year round. Facilities here include restaurants, shops, toilets, visitor centers and campsites. The large numbers of visitors mean that a summer day may feature 6,000 vehicles trying to drive along the South Rim. This number is three times the number of parking places available, which leads to long lines and pollution from idling car engines. In summer, pollution is also blown into the park from Los Angeles, which can cause the wonderful view of the Canyon to be obscured by haze. Visitors to the Grand Canyon are in danger of "loving it to death."

NATIONAL PARKS

Mt Ranier

Crater Lake

Redwood

Yellowstone

Capital Reef

Arches

Bryce Canyon

Canyonlands

Yosemite

Zion

Grand Canyon

Sequoia

Petrified Forest

Isle Royale

Mammoth Cave

Big Bend

Everglades

HAWAII

Denali

Wrangell-St-Elias

ALASKA

Hawaii Volcanoes

The National Park Service has taken the following steps to protect the park from human impact:

- The West Rim can only be accessed by shuttle bus.
- There is a park-and-ride system in the nearest town to the Canyon.
- A new public transport system is planned for within the park.

- Flights over the Canyon are limited in certain areas because of noise frightening the animals.
- Rangers give talks to make people aware of their impacts on the Canyon.

By carrying out these developments the National Park Service aims to ensure that the Grand Canyon remains in its natural state for future generations.

The deep, water-cut valleys of Grand Canyon National Park, in Arizona.

THE ENVIRONMENT

Pollution in the air gives this sunset in Los Angeles its orange color.

The United States is a consumer society with a high standard of living. It uses huge amounts of energy and produces vast amounts of waste. As a largely urban society, it is dependent on the automobile for the majority of its transport. All of these factors have an effect on the natural environment.

Carbon emissions from homes and industries add to the percentage of carbon dioxide in the atmosphere, which leads to global warming. Other gases released into the atmosphere help create acid rain, and the acidification of rivers and lakes in areas such as the Appalachians and New Jersey.

Air pollution is a problem in most US cities, particularly in Los Angeles, where smog appears on a daily basis. Due to its location, Los Angeles often experiences a temperature inversion, in which warm air overlies cold air. Harmful gases build up from car exhausts within this cold, stable layer. When they react with sunlight, they produce low-level ozone, a harmful irritant that can cause lung problems. When the temperature inversion is finally broken down by winds, the air pollution can travel inland and form a haze in the Grand Canyon, obscuring the view.

CASE STUDY
CHESAPEAKE BAY

Chesapeake Bay is the country's largest estuary, situated on the east coast. The water in the bay is a mixture of salt water from the Atlantic Ocean and fresh water from the rivers that drain into it. This leads to a variety of ecosystems, depending on the level of salinity at a particular location. Huge numbers of fish, shellfish and birds used to live in the bay. At one time, oysters could filter the entire waters of the bay in just a few days. Now the process takes over a year.

Human settlement has caused changes in Chesapeake Bay. Over 15 million people now live in the catchment areas of the rivers that drain into it and along the coast. One problem is excessive nutrients, which find their way into the bay from agricultural run-offs and from sewage works. Both sources produce nitrates and phosphates, which encourage the growth of algae. These organisms block out light to the lower depths of water, and some plants die as a result. When the algae die they sink to the bottom. As they decompose, oxygen is taken from the water. Some species of fish and other organisms cannot survive in the reduced oxygen levels, so they swim elsewhere or die.

A fisherman brings in his catch of blue crabs from the waters of Chesapeake Bay.

Water in the bay is less clear than it used to be. Cutting down upstream forests for agriculture has caused a great deal of sediment to flow into the bay every year, and plants such as eel grass cannot survive. If the grasses die, the water becomes even cloudier because the grasses help to trap sediment. They also slow down the movement of waves, thus protecting the coastline from erosion. In the growing season, the grasses also absorb large amounts of nitrates and phosphates. Numbers of geese and other birds have gone down because they are dependent on the declining grasses for food.

Fish and shellfish are also suffering because of over-harvesting. The removal of large numbers of shellfish means that the natural filtration system of the bay is being severely reduced.

In 1983, the Chesapeake Bay Agreement was drawn up. Its aim is to restore wildlife in the bay by dealing first with water quality. There has been a ban on the use of phosphate-based detergents throughout the area, and an education campaign has informed the public about its impact on the bay's ecosystem. Farmers are encouraged to minimize nitrate fertilizer use. The target of the agreement is to reduce excess nutrients by 40 percent, and to continue to restore damaged habitats.

THE AMERICAN CITIZEN AND THE ENVIRONMENT

Although US citizens use more resources per person than does any other nation, they are still concerned about their environment. The first national park was created in the United States and Americans are eager to conserve their landscapes for future generations. As people become more educated about environmental issues, they are more aware of their own impacts on the environment.

ENVIRONMENTAL ORGANIZATIONS

There are many environmental organizations, both at a national and local level. One of the most well-known national organizations is the Sierra Club, which was founded in 1892. Today it counts 600,000 members. The club's aims include education to help protect and restore environments, and the responsible use of the earth's ecosystems and resources.

At the local level, many groups were set up as a result of the 1992 Rio Earth Summit's call to "Think globally, act locally." These groups work on projects such as tree planting, organizing litter-collection days, or developing environmental awareness in their area.

ADOPT-A-HIGHWAY SCHEME

The Adopt-a-Highway program operates across the entire country. Citizens, businesses or organizations "adopt" a stretch of highway for a period of one or two years. A sign is erected at the side of the road to indicate which group is responsible for a particular stretch of highway, and the group keeps its area litter-free and tidy. In California there are more than 6,000 groups who keep more than 9,000km of roads clean. Their combined labor has been worth $140 billion since the scheme began in the 1980s, which has allowed the authorities to concentrate their money on road repairs and improvements instead of litter collection.

RECYCLING

Recycling banks exist throughout the country and are very common in California. In some areas residents are expected to sort their trash into glass, paper, plastic or organic wastes, which have separate banks. The lack of landfill space in which to place trash means the authorities want to recycle more and to encourage firms to use less packaging in order to reduce the waste going into landfill sites.

TRANSPORT

Americans are highly dependent on their cars, which creates a huge demand for oil and pollutes the atmosphere with emissions. In California the four-lane highways are often completely blocked during rush hours. Along many sections there is now an extra lane, called the carpool lane, which can only be accessed by cars containing more than one person. This lane is less congested than the other lanes, so it encourages people to share their cars by allowing them to reach their destinations faster. The fewer cars on the road, the less damage to the environment. However, even during rush hours, the carpool lane is often underused, showing that more needs to be done to encourage car sharing.

The far left-hand lane on the Los Angeles freeway can be used only by drivers with more than one person in their car.

ACTION GROUPS

Numerous action groups campaign on a single issue in the United States. The Glen Canyon Action Network (GCAN) was set up to prevent further damage to the Colorado River and to try to reverse some of the damage already done. In 1963, a large dam was built on the Colorado and the Glen Canyon was flooded behind it, creating Lake Powell. The costs of the dam construction and maintenance have not yet been covered by the benefits of electricity production from the dam. The dam has also damaged the river's ecosystems and this, combined with its costs, has led the GCAN to campaign for the demolition of the dam, the draining of Lake Powell and the restoration of the spectacular Glen Canyon.

A row of recycling bins for bottles (called bottle banks) in California.

A SUSTAINABLE FUTURE?

To develop sustainably, a country must use its resources without affecting the needs of future generations. At present, within the United States, this is not the case. The growing population is using more energy and resources than ever before.

American cars are more efficient today, but there are more of them. In California alone there are 22 million cars, which leads to congestion on the roads and a drain on fuel reserves. The country emits more greenhouse gases per person than does any other nation. These gases include carbon dioxide, methane and nitrous oxides, which are emitted from car exhausts, industries, power stations and domestic heating systems. The amount is linked to the high standard of living enjoyed by the average American, but there are not enough fuel reserves to sustain this level of use.

KYOTO

In 1998 the United States signed the Kyoto Protocol, and agreed to reduce its greenhouse gas emissions by 5 percent by the year 2010. In June 2001, soon after he was elected president, President George W. Bush withdrew from this agreement because he thought it would damage the country's economy. This decision has separated the United States from the majority of other developed nations, who are using the target set by Kyoto as the minimum they should try to achieve. Americans have a mixed view. A poll conducted in March 2001 showed that citizens thought in a more sustainable way than their government, and were more in tune with the other developed nations of the world. When asked the best way to solve the country's energy crisis, 56 percent responded that the solution should center upon conservation, in which people use less energy and therefore produce less carbon dioxide. California leads the way in reducing the amounts of energy used by each citizen, and with government help these ideas could be implemented by other states to reduce greenhouse gas emissions.

Demonstrators in June 2001 protest against President Bush's decision to withdraw the United States from agreements to reduce its greenhouse gas emissions.

CHALLENGES

Police and firefighters begin the long and distressing job of cleaning up after the attack on the World Trade Center.

At times the United States has been unwilling to become involved in international affairs. This changed forever on 11 September 2001, when the World Trade Center and the Pentagon were bombed by terrorists flying hijacked planes.

THE WORLD'S LOSS

In just minutes more than 3,000 people were killed in the suicide attacks. The exact number will never be known, as many bodies were impossible to identify. Although most of the dead were Americans, people of many other nationalities, including several hundred British citizens, were also killed. Almost the entire world was horrified by what had happened; one of the few people to praise the bombers was Osama bin Laden, who was soon identified as the likely leader of the terrorist plot.

THE UNITED STATES RESPONDS

Very quickly President Bush began to organize an alliance of the world's nations to fight the terrorist threat. One of his closest allies was British Prime Minister Tony Blair, who travelled around the world to persuade national leaders to join the alliance. The allies began a campaign against Afghanistan and its ruling party, the Taliban, who were sheltering bin Laden and refusing to release him for trial. Bombing raids were followed by attacks by small groups of alliance soldiers. By early 2002 the alliance had pushed the Taliban from power, but by March they still had not captured bin Laden. No one was sure whether he had escaped or been killed in the bombing raids.

At the same time, the United States wanted to widen the battle against terrorism with campaigns against other countries. Many of the nation's European allies disagreed with this aim, fearing it would spark more violence.

GLOSSARY

Acid rain Rain that contains sulphuric and nitric acids, produced by burning fossil fuels and absorbed by the clouds from the air.

Barrier island A low, sandy bank that develops off gently sloping coasts.

Biomass power Energy produced from plant material or vegetation.

Convection currents Currents caused by the expansion of a gas or a liquid when its temperature rises. In the semi-solid rock of the earth's mantle, convection currents cause the plates to move.

Delta A triangular-shaped area of land near the mouths of some rivers where sediment is deposited by rivers as they meet the sea.

Distributaries The branches of rivers that flow away from the main stream.

Drainage basin The area that is drained by a river and its tributaries.

Ecosystems Communities of animals and plants, and the environments in which they live.

Emissions Waste gases and solids discharged into the air from factory chimneys and vehicle exhausts.

Epicenter The point on the surface of the earth directly above the focus of an earthquake.

Estuary The part of a river that broadens into the sea.

Fossil fuels Fuels that have formed over millions of years and have been preserved, or fossilized. The main fossil fuels are coal, oil and gas.

Global warming The gradual warming of the surface of the planet as a result of a change in the composition of atmospheric gases, especially an increase in the percentage of carbon dioxide.

Greenhouse gases Gases that help to trap warmth in the atmosphere, which contributes to global warming.

Gross Domestic Product (GDP) The total value of goods produced by a country's economy.

Gross National Product (GNP) The total value of goods produced by industry and services within a country and earned by that country abroad.

Hi-tech industries High technology industries, which use the latest production techniques and technology, such as aerospace, computing and electronics.

Hurricane Violent tropical storm that forms over warm seas. The high-speed winds spiral around a central calm area called the eye.

Immigrant A person who moves away from his or her home country to settle permanently in another.

Industrial base The main types of work providing income for an economy.

Levee A bank at the side of a river that has been naturally formed when the river has overflowed and dropped sediment.

Permafrost A layer of permanently frozen soil, found near the surface of the arctic regions.

Plain A large area of flat land.

Plate One of several sections of the earth's crust composed of rock several kilometers thick, which can be thousands of kilometers wide.

Plateau A raised area of relatively flat land.

Prairie A large area of land with grass and few or no trees.

Private investment Money from individuals rather than companies.

Rain shadow An area on the leeward side of a mountain range that receives little rainfall because most has already fallen on the windward side.

Recession A time when the level of economic activity declines and unemployment and poverty levels rise.

Richter scale A scale used to measure the magnitude of an earthquake.

Spit A ridge of sand or shingle that projects out into the sea. It is joined to the land at one end.

Spur A ridge or hill that projects from the main mass of land.

Tax incentives A method used by governments to encourage people to produce or buy something by reducing the tax they have to pay on it.

Tornado A violent revolving storm formed over rapidly heated land.

Trading deficit The amount by which a sum of money falls short.

Tributary A stream or river that flows into the main channel of a river.

Tundra A high latitude region where it is too cold for trees to grow. The vegetation consists of lichens, mosses and grasses.

FURTHER INFORMATION

BOOKS TO READ:

Baines, John. *Country Fact Files: The United States.* Milwaukee, WI: Raintree Publishers, 1994. Illustrated reference for ages 12 and up.

Brogan, Hugh. *The Penguin History of the USA.* New York: Penguin USA, 2001. An overview of the entire history of the United States.

Cook, Samantha, Tim Perry and Greg Ward. *The Rough Guide to the USA.* London: Rough Guides, Ltd., 2002. A comprehensive handbook to the United States, with practical tips and commentary.

Guiness, Paul and Brian Price. *North America: An Advanced Geography.* London: Hodder & Stoughton Educational Division, 1997. Textbook for high school students, covering both the United States and Canada.

MacDonald, Chris and Jon Nichol. *Modern America.* London: Stanley Thornes Publishers, Ltd., 1996. Textbook covering US history since 1914.

Phillipson, Olly. *Country Studies: United States.* Crystal Lake, IL: Heinemann Library, 2000. Illustrated reference for young adults.

Whittock, Martyn. *The Native Peoples of North America.* London: Hodder & Stoughton Educational Division, 2002. Textbook for students ages 12 and up, covering the history and cultural diversity of indigenous North American peoples.

WEBSITES:

Labor Statistics: http://www.bls.gov/data/

Rivers: http://www.americanrivers.org

Transport: http://www.bts.gov

PEOPLE
Census data: http://www.census.gov

The Navajo Nation:
http://www.americanwest.com/pages/navajo2.htm

GENERAL INFORMATION ON THE UNITED STATES
General Information on all states:
http://www.globalcomputing.com/states.html

News Updates: http://www.cnn.com

Energy and the Environment:
http://www.eia.doe.gov/

National Park Service: http://www.nps.gov

METRIC CONVERSION TABLE

To convert	to	do this
mm (millimeters)	inches	divide by 25.4
cm (centimeters)	inches	divide by 2.54
m (meters)	feet	multiply by 3.281
m (meters)	yards	multiply by 1.094
km (kilometers)	yards	multiply by 1094
km (kilometers)	miles	divide by 1.6093
kilometers per hour	miles per hour	divide by 1.6093
cm^2 (square centimeters)	square inches	divide by 6.452
m^2 (square meters)	square feet	multiply by 10.76
m^2 (square meters)	square yards	multiply by 1.196
km^2 (square kilometers)	square miles	divide by 2.59
km^2 (square kilometers)	acres	multiply by 247.1
hectares	acres	multiply by 2.471
cm^3 (cubic centimeters)	cubic inches	multiply by 16.387
m^3 (cubic meters)	cubic yards	multiply by 1.308
l (liters)	pints	multiply by 2.113
l (liters)	gallons	divide by 3.785
g (grams)	ounces	divide by 28.329
kg (kilograms)	pounds	multiply by 2.205
metric tonnes	short tons	multiply by 1.1023
metric tonnes	long tons	multiply by 0.9842
BTUs (British thermal units)	kWh (kilowatt-hours)	divide by 3,415.3
watts	horsepower	multiply by 0.001341
kWh (kilowatt-hours)	horsepower-hours	multiply by 1.341
MW (megawatts)	horsepower	multiply by 1,341
gigawatts per hour	horsepower per hour	multiply by 1,341,000
°C (degrees Celsius)	°F (degrees Fahrenheit)	multiply by 1.8 then add 32

INDEX

The Statue of Liberty, New York City.

Manhattan, New York City,
at sunset.